MEMORIZATION FOR ACTORS

ALEXA ISPAS

WORD
BOTHY

CONTENTS

INTRODUCTION

Are you an actor who struggles to remember lines and finds the process of memorization frustrating?

Or do you already have a relatively successful memorization process, but would like to make it even better?

Either way, this book is designed to help you learn your lines faster and more reliably than ever before.

This is a bold claim, so let me explain why I feel confident making it.

Although I have written this book specifically for actors, the strategies I will introduce to you do not come from the world of acting.

They come from hundreds of research studies in psychology.

Over several decades, psychological studies into memory have provided a huge amount of insight into how memory works.

This is the first book of its kind to adapt these insights to actors' memorization requirements.

I believe that if actors were shown how to take advantage of psychological research into memory, they could memorize their lines quicker and more reliably than ever before.

I am not an actress myself. My background is in psychology, a subject I have studied to PhD level and absolutely adore.

But I'm also a free spirit, and for years I pursued acting as an alternative career option.

I eventually realized I didn't love acting enough to make it a lifelong occupation.

However, during my foray into acting, I witnessed first-hand the mistakes actors make while learning their lines.

I also saw the huge amount of frustration, stress, and stage-fright that come with not being entirely confident of knowing your lines.

I am convinced that providing actors with a better understanding of how their memory works will resolve these problems.

This book offers specific tools actors can use to

learn their lines quicker and more reliably than their current standard.

In addition, the book will introduce you to a highly effective memorization process.

This process is based on solid psychological evidence of how to make the most of your memory capacity.

Once established, this process will allow you to memorize more material than ever before, in less time, and with reliable results regardless of circumstances.

By the time you finish this book, you will have a wide range of memorization strategies up your sleeve.

You will also understand *why* they work and *when* to use each of them for maximum effect.

Understanding *why* particular strategies work will give you confidence that you are spending your memorization time productively.

This certainty will make learning lines motivating and fun.

Memorization will no longer be a chore you must undertake, or a task you find frustrating due to not being able to rely on the results.

Enjoying the process of memorization, and

trusting in its reliability, will have many benefits to your acting career.

You will need less time to prepare for auditions, and therefore be able to take advantage of opportunities even if they come up at short notice.

You will also feel more confident during auditions, allowing directors and members of the casting team to see the real you.

Once you get the part, directors will love working with you because of how well prepared you will be.

This will put you miles ahead of the competition and lead to more work opportunities further down the line.

There is one caveat to all these benefits: you have to put this memorization process into practice.

If you are not willing to do that, this book won't be of any use to you, and there's no point in buying it.

But if you are prepared to put in your side of the bargain, I'm delighted to have you on board.

I have kept this book short, so you can read it in an afternoon and have a detailed memorization process by the time you finish.

The book will provide you with everything you

need to know about how memory works that is relevant to learning lines.

Each chapter focuses on one specific aspect of memorization that is important to your final, overall process.

I have also provided a summary at the end of each chapter, for a quick reminder of the key points.

The final chapter brings everything together into a step-by-step memorization process, so you can refer to it any time you get stuck.

And now, without further ado, allow me to introduce you to the weird and wonderful features of your own memory.

CHAPTER 1

THE COMPLEX NATURE OF MEMORY

SHORT-TERM AND LONG-TERM MEMORY

We generally talk about 'memory' as if it was a single entity.

However, all the available psychological evidence suggests that what we refer to as 'memory' is in fact made up of several systems and processes.

Two memory systems are particularly relevant to the process of learning lines.

I will refer to them as 'short-term memory' and 'long-term memory'.

Each of these plays a crucial role in memorization.

LEARNING LINES USING SHORT-TERM MEMORY

Short-term memory holds those items in our minds that we need to perform the task at hand.

As you are reading this text, you are using your short-term memory to remember the previous sentence, so the sentence you are reading at the moment makes sense.

As this example illustrates, we use short-term memory continuously in daily life, often without realizing it.

It is thanks to short-term memory that we can remember a telephone number long enough to dial it.

Short-term memory has many uses while you are in the process of learning your lines.

For example, it allows you to read a line of text and remember it long enough to say it without looking back at the text.

This is an ability you may often use in the early stages of memorization.

Short-term memory is also invaluable in certain types of auditions.

For example, you need your short-term memory in situations when you are given your line just minutes before being asked to say it in front of the casting team or the camera.

Actors who work for film or television often rely on their short-term memory when they are given their script the night before or on the morning of the audition or shoot.

In such circumstances, there is no time to go through the full process of learning lines.

Short-term memory helps you reproduce the lines without having them fully memorized.

The reason short-term memory enables you to say the lines so soon after you have been exposed to them is that it keeps them immediately accessible.

As long as the lines are held in your short-term memory, you can say them.

You do not need the time-consuming process of storing the lines in long-term memory.

Even more astonishingly, short-term memory allows you to memorize words and lines even if you do not understand their meaning.

Indeed, the ability to learn foreign languages rests on this feature of short-term memory.

You can simply repeat a word or phrase you have just heard even before you know what it means.

This is because, as studies have shown, short-term memory stores information using a so-called 'acoustic code'.

It encodes the information based on the sounds you hear.

This makes it possible to reproduce your lines from short-term memory despite not understanding their meaning.

THE LIMITATIONS OF SHORT-TERM MEMORY

For all its amazing capabilities, short-term memory presents actors with some serious limitations when learning lines.

One limitation is that, as the name suggests, it only holds the material for a short amount of time.

This can be as little as a few seconds, unless the material is continuously repeated to keep it active.

Actors are sometimes astounded at the speed with which they can learn a piece of text, only to realize minutes later that the lines have gone.

You therefore need to be careful not to confuse holding the lines in short-term memory with actually having learned the lines.

The neural connections that support short-term memory prioritize new information over existing information.

This is why you can only hold lines in your short-term memory for a short amount of time.

The material held in your short-term memory is unstable.

How long you can keep material in your short-term memory depends on whether any new material displaces it.

As long as you can keep your lines at the fore-front of your mind, you can remember them.

However, as soon as you allow your attention to drift to something else, you risk forgetting the lines.

Indeed, even having to say 'hello' to the casting team, or the director calling 'action', can make you forget the lines if you are relying on your short-term memory alone.

To memorize lines reliably, you need your other memory system: long-term memory.

LEARNING LINES USING LONG-TERM MEMORY

For line learning, long-term memory is infinitely more reliable than short-term memory.

This is because the material is maintained by more stable neural connections in your brain, ideally suited for the task of holding information long-term.

Once the lines are lodged in your long-term memory, they are much less vulnerable to the effects of distractions or other external factors.

However, before reaching this stage, two problems must be overcome.

The first problem is that before lines can become embedded in your long-term memory, they must be processed by your short-term memory.

However, this is not simply a matter of shifting the material from one container to another.

Unlike long-term memory, which has unlimited capacity, the capacity of short-term memory is extremely limited.

As such, short-term memory works like a bottleneck.

If you are not mindful of the restrictions imposed by this bottleneck, the liquid you are trying to pour into the bottle will spill.

Memorizing lines, whether short- or long-term, therefore depends on the way you use your short-term memory capacity.

The second problem is that while the lines are reliably stored in your long-term memory, your success in using them depends on how easily you can retrieve them.

To illustrate, here is a situation you have probably encountered in your daily life: forgetting a familiar name just as you are about to introduce the person to someone else.

In this case, the problem is not that the name was only stored in your short-term memory and is now gone.

If it is a familiar name, it is by definition lodged in your long-term memory and is still safely stored away.

Instead, the problem in this instance is that you are having trouble retrieving the name from your long-term memory.

The same can happen with your lines.

Fortunately for actors, there are solutions to both problems related to storing lines in long-term memory.

This book will provide you with the understanding and specific tools to develop a bullet-proof memorization process that overcomes these problems.

This process will allow you to learn your lines quicker and more reliably than ever before.

KEY POINTS

- Learning lines depends on two distinct memory systems: short-term memory and long-term memory. Each of these systems plays its part in a different way.
- Short-term memory provides immediate access to the material, but only allows you to memorize lines for a short amount of time.
- This system is also susceptible to distractions and has a limited storage capacity.
- Long-term memory has unlimited capacity, but to make use of it you must first transfer the material from short-term memory, which acts as a bottleneck.
- Once the material is stored in long-term memory, you must also be able to easily retrieve the material.

- Learning lines depends on two factors: (1) successfully transferring the lines from short-term into long-term memory; (2) being able to easily retrieve the lines from long-term memory.

—

CHAPTER 2

DISMANTLING THE 'POOR MEMORY' BELIEF

A SELF-FULFILLING PROPHECY

Before we get into the nitty-gritty of developing a memorization process, I wanted to address a common self-sabotaging belief.

This is the belief, held by some actors, that their memory is not as good as everyone else's.

During my acting days, I witnessed first-hand how debilitating it was when actors believed this about themselves.

The problem with this belief is that it becomes a self-fulfilling prophecy.

If you believe your memory is poor, your motivation for learning your lines is likely to be low.

You may therefore put too little time and effort into learning your lines, as you don't trust your memory.

You may also postpone learning your lines until it is too late, adding an extra layer of stress to an already stressful situation.

The result is that you will turn up to auditions unprepared, and your lack of confidence is likely to lead to a poor performance.

BELIEF VS RESEARCH EVIDENCE

If you happen to hold even a tiny shred of this belief, please allow me to provide reassurance: your memory is just as good as everyone else's.

In fact, unless you suffer from dementia or anything similar, there is no such thing as having 'poor memory'.

If you have read the first chapter, you will know that in order to store the lines in your long-term memory, you first have to hold them in your short-term memory.

This is because short-term memory acts like a bottleneck.

The interesting thing in relation to the 'poor

memory' belief is that all adults have the same short-term memory capacity of around seven items.

This means that you can only hold around seven items in your short-term memory at any one time.

However, the good news is that your memory is just as good as that of any other actor out there.

Even those actors who seem to rattle off reams of text at the drop of a hat?

Yes, even those.

I will show you in later chapters how that kind of memorization prowess is possible, despite the limitations short-term memory places on all of us.

For now, I would like to convince you, once and for all, that there is no such thing as suffering from a 'poor memory'.

The more certain you become that your memory is just as good as everyone else's, the more motivated you will be to put serious effort into learning your lines.

Let us take a closer look at the facts.

THE SEVEN ITEM LIMIT

The seven-item limit of short-term memory is easily demonstrated through the 'memory span task'.

In this task, which you may have seen as part of TV game shows, participants listen to a series of items.

They must repeat these items in order after hearing them only once.

Studies using the 'memory span task' found that if the items are randomly chosen letters or digits, people can remember around seven items without any problem.

However, when participants are presented with more than seven items, the number of mistakes sharply increases.

This seven item limit has been replicated across a wide number of studies involving many different people.

For actors, this means that even those who appear to have phenomenal memories do not.

The limited capacity of short-term memory is the big equalizer.

This is good news if you think you suffer from having a poor memory.

Any actor can achieve great memory feats as long as they are prepared to put in the work and use an efficient memorization system, such as the one outlined in this book.

No matter what negative beliefs you may have held in the past about your memory, you have the potential to become an expert at learning your lines quickly and reliably.

As we will see in the next few chapters, what differentiates those whom we regard as having 'excellent memory' from the rest is that they use a highly effective memorization process.

This process allows them to make the most of the limitations imposed by their short-term memory.

KEY POINTS

- The 'poor memory' belief is debilitating for actors and becomes a self-fulfilling prophecy.
- In fact, research evidence shows that all adults have the same short-term memory capacity of around seven items.

- The limited capacity of short-term memory is the big equalizer. Your memory is just as good as everyone else's.
- To make the most of your short-term memory capacity, you need an efficient memorization system.

CHAPTER 3

ACHIEVING MEMORIZATION EXCELLENCE

THE MYSTERY OF MEMORY GENIUS

In the previous chapter, we have seen evidence that we all have the same short-term memory capacity of around seven items.

But if this is the case, how is it possible for some people to achieve extraordinary memory feats with information that has just been presented to them?

You have probably come across such sensational displays of short-term memory 'genius'.

Do these cases not contradict the seven-item limit we have just discussed?

They do not.

As we will see, people who achieve such

extraordinary memory feats do not rely on their short-term memory alone.

They have found a clever way of also making use of their long-term memory.

In this chapter, we will take a closer look at these people.

Their memory accomplishments can teach us how to make the most of the seven-item limit of short-term memory.

We will then apply this to the process of learning lines.

THE MEMORY FEATS OF CHESS EXPERTS

One group of people who display extraordinary memory feats are expert chess players.

For example, there are chess players who can play ten simultaneous games blindfolded.

How are they able to do this?

If the chess players were holding all those chess board configurations in short-term memory, they would fail.

As already mentioned, short-term memory is susceptible to distractions.

As such, if they relied on their short-term memory alone, the chess players would get continuously distracted and be unable to focus on their game.

At the same time, it would take too long to transfer all that information into long-term storage to be able to play the game.

Research examining this puzzle suggests that these expert chess players have developed, over their many years of playing, a special system.

This system combines the best features of short-term and long-term memory.

It allows the players to anchor the new chess configurations they are encountering to similar material that is already held in their long-term memory.

Due to this anchoring to long-term memory material, the new chess configurations can withstand the disruption of shifting between different games.

This allows the chess experts to make use of the new configurations as they require.

As such, it is not that these chess players have a greater short-term memory capacity than everyone else.

It is just that over time, they have developed the capacity to use their long-term memory faster.

This allows them to remember new information by making it 'stick' to information that is already available in their long-term memory.

As we will see, this is something that is common to all displays of memory prowess, and is particularly relevant to the process of learning lines.

For now, I would just like to point out one other aspect of this research on expert chess players: their extraordinary memory feats only apply to chess.

Outside this area, they handle any memory task in the same way as the rest of us.

This shows that in general, their memory is average.

Their accomplishments when it comes to chess are based on their expertise, acquired over many years of practice.

FROM AVERAGE TO GREAT MEMORY

What about ordinary people, including actors?

Can someone who is not an expert in a particular field acquire the necessary memory skills used by experts?

In the 1970s, a team of researchers began

examining this question using the so-called 'digit span task'.

The task consists of listening to random digits (e.g. 7, 1, 3, 5, 2) presented at a rate of one per second.

After a delay of 20 seconds, the participant has to remember the entire sequence.

If the recall is correct, the sequence gets increased by one digit.

If the recall is incorrect, it gets decreased by one digit.

The number of digits the participant is able to remember as part of this task is called their 'digit span'.

The study reported the extraordinary memory feats of Steve Faloon, a participant who began the study just like everyone else.

His initial 'digit span' was seven digits, as you would expect from having read about the limits of short-term memory.

However, Faloon gradually became a virtuoso at recalling digits.

By the end of the study, Faloon's digit span had reached an amazing 82 digits.

It is worth illustrating just how extraordinary Steve Faloon's achievement was.

Imagine that someone is reading you the following series of numbers at a rate of one digit per second: 4 9 8 3 9 8 7 4 3 5 9 8 7 6 9 9 7 3 4 8 7 6 2 3 4 8 7 6 2 3 6 1 7 6 5 1 2 9 8 2 5 9 7 3 2 9 8 7 6 4 3 7 6 5 1 6 7 5 3 2 1 7 6 4 2 0 4 2 3 8 7 6 3 2 8 7 6 3 2 0 7 8.

Your task is to start reproducing the digits in the exact order in which they were presented, 20 seconds after the last digit was read out.

You only hear the numbers once.

How did Steve Faloon achieve this extraordinary feat of memory?

The digit span task is not like a chessboard.

Unlike chess experts, he would not be able to apply board positions stored in long-term memory to help him maximize his short-term memory capacity.

Nevertheless, here is where it gets interesting, and where we need to think about how this applies to learning lines.

The study revealed that the method Steve Faloon developed bore a strong resemblance to the one used by the expert chess players.

First of all, he worked hard, and he set about his task patiently.

He was only able to achieve the 82 digits after

devoting more than 250 hours to this task over many months.

This consistent effort, just like the chess players, turned him into an expert at this particular task.

Secondly, just like the expert chess players, Steve Faloon's system consisted of relating the digits in his short-term memory to knowledge that was available in his long-term memory.

He was a successful track and cross-country runner and was therefore familiar with timed runs.

He used this knowledge to remember the digits.

For example, he recalled the digits 4 1 3 1 in the form 4:13.1, a time for running the mile.

He also recalled the digits 9 4 6 2 as 9 minutes, 46.2 seconds, a time for running two miles.

Similarly to the chess players, Steve Faloon's extraordinary short-term memory accomplishment was not based on an initial above-average memory capacity.

As already mentioned, his initial 'digit span' was only seven digits, just like everyone else.

His success was based on using pre-existing knowledge available in his long-term memory to make the most of his short-term memory capacity.

It is also important to mention that his extraordinary memory improvement when it came to digits did not transfer to anything else.

For example, when he was tested on random letters, his 'memory span task' was seven, the same as for most people.

What allowed him to perform so well in the digit span task was the consistent effort applied to this task and the efficient memorization system he employed.

DEVELOPING LINE LEARNING EXPERTISE

There are a few important things we can learn from these studies of extraordinary memory feats.

In particular, I would like to note a few similarities between the chess experts and Steve Faloon, as these are things we can also apply to learning lines.

The first similarity is that neither the chess players nor Steve Faloon possessed an above-average memory in general.

Their extraordinary memory feats were due to their consistent practice and their expertise in a particular area, rather than to above-average natural abilities.

This is worth emphasizing.

You still need to put in the effort and the time to learn your lines, even with the best memorization process in the world.

There are no short-cuts when it comes to learning your lines.

The second similarity is that despite both the chess experts and Steve Faloon being required to remember new information quickly, they did not rely on their short-term memory alone.

Instead, they both heavily involved their long-term memory.

They used what they already knew to boost their short-term memory performance.

Steve Faloon also used 'chunking' (organizing individual items into bigger units) to increase the number of digits he could remember.

Chunking is a powerful way of speeding up the memorization process and is easily transferrable to learning lines.

We will discuss the use of chunking in more depth in a later chapter.

Finally, both the chess experts and Steve Faloon had a powerful asset that allowed them to turn an average memory capacity into an extraordinary memorization machine.

I am referring to their memorization process, without which all their hard work would have been far less effective.

As you keep reading this book, you will gather a set of tools for your own memorization process.

KEY POINTS

- Studies of people who have accomplished extraordinary feats of memory can teach us how to overcome the limitations of short-term memory.
- These studies show that the extraordinary memory feats are not based on any remarkable memory ability.
- The memory achievements are due to developing the ability to use information stored in long-term memory to boost short-term memory performance.
- One of the studies also demonstrated the use of 'chunking' (organizing individual items into larger units) to

increase the amount of material held in short-term memory.

- What differentiates those whom we regard as having 'excellent memory' from the rest is the process they use to make the most of their short-term memory limitations.

CHAPTER 4

THE PITFALLS OF LINE LEARNING

BAD MEMORIZATION HABITS

In the previous chapter, we looked into studies of extraordinary memory accomplishments.

These studies allowed us to distill a few important points that apply to learning lines.

However, learning lines is different from remembering chess board configurations, or memorizing digits like Steve Faloon.

The good news is that learning lines is generally easier than the memorization tasks we considered in the previous chapter.

One important way in which learning lines is easier is that actors have the luxury of time.

This applies even if they are only given the

script a few hours before the audition or other type of performance.

That is still more time than either the chess players or Steve Faloon had as part of their memorization tasks.

However, having time to learn lines is only an advantage if that time is spent productively.

Many actors do not know how to make best use of the time they have available.

They do not have a carefully crafted memorization process to call upon, such as the one you will find in the final chapter of this book.

Instead, actors generally rely on habits they developed in their early acting days.

If they picked up good habits during that time, they may find memorization easy despite not having consciously given it much thought.

However, not all actors are so lucky.

One bad habit some actors get into is to attempt to memorize their lines by absent-mindedly reading their script over and over.

They do so in the hope that with enough repetition, they will eventually remember their lines.

Intuitively, they sense that repetition enables the transition from short-term into long-term memory.

However, absent-minded repetition presents actors with two big problems.

The first problem is that this type of repetition does not lead to memorization.

Studies have demonstrated the futility of repeating material over and over without engaging with it.

These studies have conclusively shown that if the repetition was done absent-mindedly, the length of time spent repeating the material provided little to no benefit for memorization.

As such, how long you have spent reading your lines in an absent-minded way is not a good indication of how well you have memorized them.

The second problem is that while absent-minded repetition is useless for the purpose of memorization, it does often lead to recognition.

This means you are able to recognize your lines and know what comes next, as long as you have the text in front of you.

For example, you experience recognition when you start reading a book, only to realize you already know what comes next as you've read it before.

However, recognition is not the same as memorization.

To remember your lines through recognition, you only need to process them at a superficial level.

You have the feeling of déjà vu as soon as you read them, leading to a false sense that you already know the text.

Many actors who are in the habit of absent-mindedly reading their script over and over fall into the recognition trap.

They think they have memorized their lines simply because they know what comes next while re-reading them.

They do not realize they have not even started the process of memorization, and are shocked to find themselves unprepared when they enter the audition room.

It is no wonder so many actors find the process of memorization time-consuming and frustrating.

This also explains why the 'poor memory' belief is alive and well among actors, despite scientific evidence that everybody has the same memory capacity.

HOW TO REPEAT YOUR LINES DURING MEMORIZATION

If you want to learn your lines quickly and reliably, you need to keep your brain actively engaged while you keep repeating them.

Each time you actively engage with your lines, you are allowing the material to transfer from your short-term to your long-term memory.

You are also making the lines easier to retrieve when it matters.

What does actively engaging with your lines mean?

For one thing, it means not reading them from a script, but rather trying to say them from memory as early as possible during the memorization process.

In addition, there are many other things you can do to keep your brain actively engaged with your lines while memorizing them.

Over the next few chapters, I will introduce you to a set of tools you can use to actively engage with your lines in a variety of different ways.

Although we will discuss these tools one at a time, it is important to note that they work best when used in combination.

Those actors who are deemed to have 'excellent memories' use all of these tools, whether they are aware of it or not.

KEY POINTS

- Repetition plays a key part in memorization.
- However, not all kinds of repetition lead to successful memorization, even if you spend a long time working on your lines.
- Some actors have developed the bad habit of absent-mindedly reading their lines over and over from a script, hoping the lines will sink in through repetition.
- This absent-minded repetition of the material is ineffective, even if done for a long time.
- Actors who repeat their lines while still having the text in front of them can also be misled by the recognition trap.
- The recognition trap makes you think you know your lines simply because

you know what comes next when you have the lines in front of you.

- To truly learn your lines, you need to keep your brain actively engaged with the text throughout the memorization process.
- You also need to be able to say your lines entirely from memory instead of looking at the lines and falling into the recognition trap.

CHAPTER 5

ENGAGING WITH MEANING

MEANING AS MEMORY ANCHOR

The first and most obvious way to maintain active engagement with your lines as you repeat them is to focus on the meaning of the text.

As you work through the meaning of the lines, you are connecting your (new) lines to material that is already in your long-term memory.

By blending the new material with the old, you are making it easier to remember.

In chapter 3, we saw how well this worked for the expert chess players and Steve Faloon.

They all relied on blending new information with material stored in their long-term memory.

You can start the process of exploring the

meaning of the text by looking up unfamiliar words or phrases.

Once this is done, you can go one step further and paraphrase the text for yourself.

This will allow you to 'translate' the text into your own words and thereby make the text meaningful to you.

Just make sure that when it comes to memorizing, you learn the actual lines rather than your paraphrased version.

MEMORIZING WHEN THERE IS NO MEANING

Focusing on meaning works great for text that *has* meaning.

But what about situations where you must memorize non-sensical text, or text that appears non-sensical to you?

For example, you may be faced with a script that contains long lists of words or numbers.

Alternatively, the text may contain a made-up language, or it may be in a language you do not speak.

In such circumstances, there are alternative methods you can use.

The best-known way to remember long

stretches of non-sensical material is the 'method of loci', also called the 'memory palace'.

This method was used as far back as Ancient Greece and is still popular today.

The method consists of two steps.

The first step is to imagine a place with which you are familiar, such as your home or the street on which you live.

The second step is to go through the list of words, numbers, or other pieces of non-sensical text needing memorization.

As you go through this list, associate each item with something belonging to the location you selected.

For example, you could pair the items to be memorized with objects within your home.

In this way, the elements of your familiar location (e.g. your home, your street, or any other place you have selected) become a long-term memory 'anchor' to which you can attach the non-sensical items.

This weaving of old and new material makes the new material (including the order in which it is to be remembered) easier to remember.

Another way to deepen your engagement with non-meaningful material, which works particularly well for lists of words, is to create a memorable sentence.

This will enable you to remember the first letter of each item you must memorize.

Let's say you want to remember the colors of the rainbow: red, orange, yellow, green, blue, indigo, violet.

To do so, you would use the first letter of each to create a sentence such as 'Richard Of York Gave Battle In Vain'.

Actors rarely have to memorize such lists of words as part of their script.

However, it is a handy strategy for the few occasions where this does come up.

KEY POINTS

- The first way you can actively engage with the text as you repeat your lines is to understand its meaning.
- This includes translating the meaning for yourself through paraphrasing.
- This will help you connect the (new) lines to material you already hold in your long-term memory.

- When working with non-meaningful text, you can still relate the material to knowledge you already possess through alternative methods.
- You can use the 'method of loci' (pairing items within your text with those in a familiar location) or make a memorable sentence out of the first letter of each item.

CHAPTER 6

ORGANIZING YOUR TEXT INTO CHUNKS

THE BENEFITS OF CHUNKING

Organizing your text into chunks (or 'chunking') is another great way to maintain active engagement with your lines as you repeat them for the purpose of memorization.

This is because, as you will see, the process of chunking forces you to keep organizing and re-organizing your lines in chunks of ever-increasing size.

This constant reconfiguration makes it easy for your brain to stay engaged with the lines by keeping the chunks fresh and interesting.

In addition, chunking has two further advantages.

The first is that it speeds up your memorization process.

Every time you reconfigure your chunks, you are building new links to your lines.

As a consequence, you start seeing the results of your memorization efforts faster and can learn more lines in less time.

An even bigger advantage is that due to these additional links to the material, you are ensuring that you will remember your lines without drawing a blank.

This will be particularly helpful in situations when you have to say the lines under pressure.

Let us examine the process of chunking in more detail.

HOW CHUNKING WORKS

Even though your short-term memory can only hold around seven items, what each of these items contains is up to you.

The more material you can hold in each chunk, the more you will be able to hold in your short-term memory at any one time.

You can then gradually transfer these chunks into your long-term memory.

You are probably already using chunking in your day-to-day life without realizing it.

For example, imagine trying to remember a phone number such as 07951272566.

You are likely to chunk it into 079 51 27 25 66, or 079 512 725 66, or any such combination that works for you.

Chunking is therefore an extremely effective way of increasing the amount of material you can memorize and therefore speeding up your memorization process.

The effectiveness of chunking was demonstrated, among others, through the previously mentioned study involving Steve Faloon.

He used his experience as a long-distance runner, recoding groups of four digits as running times for various races.

Effectively, Faloon was using chunks to turn meaningless individual numbers into meaningful larger units of information.

The use of chunking allowed Faloon to turn his average short-term memory into an incredible memorization machine.

As this example shows, what counts as a chunk depends on your familiarity with the material to be memorized.

For instance, someone having to memorize material that appears devoid of meaning, such as morse code, initially hears each dot and dash as a separate chunk.

As a result, they only remember seven dots and/or dashes.

However, the more familiar this person becomes with the sounds and their sequences, the more they will be able to organize the dots and dashes into letters.

Once they can do that, they can deal with the letters as chunks.

Then they will be able to organize the letters into words, which are still larger chunks, and eventually they can begin to hear and remember whole phrases.

Studies show that anything can be memorized more effectively if it is divided up into seven or fewer chunks.

Let us see how you can apply this principle to learning lines.

THE CHUNKING PROCESS

Step 1: Divide your text into chunks

Begin by making all your lines, no matter how many there are, fit into seven chunks.

Only use your own lines for the purpose of chunking. Ignore the lines of the other actor(s) for now.

If the resulting chunks are too large to start memorizing, treat each of the chunks as a piece in itself and further divide this piece into seven (smaller) chunks.

Keep dividing up the lines into sets of seven smaller and smaller chunks until the length of each chunk feels manageable for you.

This is part of the reconfiguration process I was mentioning at the start of this chapter.

Once each of your chunks is of manageable size, start memorizing the first chunk.

Then move on to subsequent portions of your text in the same manner.

As these smaller seven-chunk pieces take hold in your long-term memory, you can gradually merge them together to form larger chunks.

Eventually, you will be able to treat the whole text, no matter how long, as one giant seven-chunk piece.

You may be amazed at how easily this initially

untamable 'monster' rolls off your tongue whenever you choose to deliver it.

Step 2: Choose a 'retrieval cue' for each chunk

You have so far divided up your lines into chunks that are short enough for you to start memorizing and have made some progress towards memorizing these chunks.

It is now time for the next stage of the process: gradually putting your chunks aside and trying to remember them from memory.

How can you make this stage of the process as effective as possible?

By setting up a so-called 'retrieval cue' for each of your chunks.

A retrieval cue is a memorable word that works the same way as a stage cue.

When the retrieval cue is called, the actor (i.e. the chunk) steps in.

A retrieval cue is therefore a short-hand version of the chunk to which it is attached.

What works well as a retrieval cue differs from person to person.

Perhaps a word you stumble upon regularly in

a particular chunk is a perfect retrieval cue for that chunk.

Once you remember that word, the rest of the chunk comes easily.

Or perhaps you could choose the first word of that chunk as your cue.

Retrieval cues can be a huge help in speeding up your memorization process.

It is therefore worth experimenting with different cues to find out which are the most effective ones for you.

Whichever word you choose as your retrieval cue for a chunk, the main point is that it should be memorable and meaningful to *you*.

The more memorable the retrieval cue, the quicker you will be able to remember the chunk to which it relates.

Choose seven retrieval cues, one for each chunk.

Make a list of your retrieval cues on a separate piece of paper.

As you attempt to remember the chunks from memory, see if you can rely on your retrieval cues, instead of looking at your chunks.

Eventually you won't need the chunks any more.

You will only need to refer to your retrieval cues.

Once you can say all the chunks with only the help of the retrieval cues, put the chunks away.

Keep your list of retrieval cues close, but not too visible.

Try saying the text without looking at your retrieval cues.

Only look at your retrieval cues when you get stuck.

Make sure that if you change the size of your chunks as you make progress with learning the lines, you remember to also change the retrieval cues relating to each chunk.

By the end, you should only have seven chunks and seven retrieval cues, no matter how long the text.

You should be able to remember your chunks easily, without needing to look at the retrieval cues.

KEY POINTS

- Chunking is a great tool to make the most of your short-term memory capacity.

- Divide any piece of text you want to memorize into seven chunks.
- If the chunks are too big, keep dividing each chunk until you end up with chunks of manageable size.
- You can then identify memorable words (or 'retrieval cues') to help you remember each chunk.
- As your memorization progresses, start combining small chunks into larger ones, until you can fit your whole text into seven chunks.
- Chunking speeds up your memorization process as it keeps your brain actively engaged with the material.
- Organizing and re-organizing your chunks while memorizing also helps you access your lines without drawing a blank, even when under pressure.

CHAPTER 7

BUILDING MULTIPLE MEMORY LINKS

BULLET-PROOFING YOUR LINES

There is nothing worse for an actor than to draw a blank in front of an audience or a casting director.

So far, in the previous two chapters, we have discussed how to set about learning your lines.

We have started with the moment you first get your script to the point where you are able to say the lines from memory.

We all hope that, once the lines are in long-term memory, we will be able to retrieve them when we need to.

However, we all know of situations when this didn't happen.

This is one of the difficulties we discussed in chapter 1.

Actors not only have to store their lines in long-term memory, they also have to be able to retrieve these lines on cue.

How can you make sure that, having memorized your lines, you are able to remember them easily, no matter how stressful the situation?

The solution is to build multiple memory links to your lines.

The more memory links you set up, the more reliably you will remember your lines, even when under stress.

To some extent, if you have been following the process up to this point, you have already started setting up multiple memory links.

You did this when you combined the two tools we have discussed so far: engaging with the meaning of the lines and dividing your text into chunks.

The reason combining these two memorization tools is so effective is that they each provide different means of accessing the lines in your memory.

The first tool, engaging with the meaning of

the lines, allows you to access them by attaching the lines to information you already know.

In most cases, you can do that by making sure you understand the meaning of the text and paraphrasing it for yourself.

Chunking, the second tool, allows you to access the lines through the way you have divided them up into chunks and the retrieval cues you have set up.

By using both tools rather than just one, you are effectively doubling your chances of accessing the material as and when you need it.

Aside from combining these two memorization tools, you can set up even more memory links to your material.

To do so, you need to set time aside to rehearse your lines in a variety of different ways.

As a minimum, I advise that you write your lines down, listen to your lines on a recording, and sing your lines.

I also advise that you say your lines as you go about your day while introducing a variety of distractions.

All the additional memory links you are building in these different ways will help you remember your lines regardless of circumstances.

Let us briefly go through each of these possibilities in turn.

WRITE THE LINES DOWN

Writing your lines engages your brain differently than saying them out loud, and therefore helps with creating additional memory links.

If possible, I suggest you write your lines at the beginning as well as towards the end of your memorization process.

At the beginning, seeing your lines in your own handwriting will add a visual memory element that will speed up your memorization process.

In addition, writing your lines slows you down and forces you to notice every single word on its own.

This is especially the case if you get stuck on a particular word or sentence.

That word or sentence will stick out more prominently in your memory as a result, and you won't forget it next time.

You may also want to write the lines towards the end, once you feel confident you are able to say them entirely from memory.

Writing them out at that point will engage your brain in a different way.

This will allow you to make sure all the lines are easily accessible and completely accurate in your memory.

As you will be using your hand to write your lines, this will also add a useful muscle memory link that will help you retrieve the lines when needed.

RECORD YOUR LINES

Recording your lines is a great addition to the memorization process.

This will allow you to listen to yourself saying your lines over and over.

The more you listen to the recording, the more the lines will become securely embedded in your long-term memory.

I suggest that you read your text while recording yourself, instead of saying your lines from memory.

That way, your recording will have a smooth flow and be completely free of hesitations.

I also suggest to make two recordings.

For the first recording, read your lines at

normal speed.

For the second recording, read them at break-neck speed.

Listen to the recordings as many times as you can.

As you get further into memorizing the text, try to say your lines from memory at the same time as the recording.

First use the normal-paced version, then move on to the fast-paced one.

Listening to the breakneck speed recording a few times every night before going to bed will help a great deal.

You will notice the results the next day, when picking up the piece again.

By listening to the recording before going to bed, you are 'delegating' the process of memorization to your subconscious.

You are therefore making it easier to remember the lines when you have to say them under pressure.

SING YOUR LINES

Singing your lines may sound strange, but it gets your brain to engage with the material in a different way than before.

As you start fitting your text around a melody, you are building additional memory links to the text.

In addition, singing your lines as part of your memorization process presents another great advantage.

When you repeat a piece of text over and over, it is natural to gradually develop a certain rhythm in the way you say the words.

This will later become a problem when it comes to acting out the words.

These patterns you have developed may keep you from responding authentically to what the other actors are doing.

Singing your lines as part of your memorization process prevents this from happening.

Having to fit the lines to a melody distracts you from the rhythms you may have developed while memorizing.

It helps you see the text in a fresh way, and gives you the freedom to be available to the truth of the moment as you start rehearsing with the other actors.

I suggest you only start singing your lines towards the end of your memorization process, once the lines are fully embedded in your long-term memory.

I also advise that you sing your lines to different tunes, to keep things fresh and playful.

INTRODUCE DISTRACTIONS

Once you fully know your lines, introduce distractions while repeating them to yourself.

Say your lines while riding a bike, doing press-ups, or any other similar physical activities.

These distractions, and the little things that happen while saying your lines, will help you build further memory links.

For example, if you almost fell off your bike while saying a particularly tricky line, you will find it easier to remember that line in the future.

Being able to say your lines with distractions will also give you confidence that you can deliver them no matter what is going on around you.

'All roads lead to Rome', as the saying goes.

Imagine if you could create so many memory links to your lines that you could remember them in an instant, regardless of circumstances.

KEY POINTS

- Setting up multiple memory links to your material entails memorizing your lines by using a variety of different mediums.
- Examples include writing your lines, recording and playing them back to yourself, and singing the lines to different tunes.
- Once you fully know your lines, introduce a variety of physical activities as distractions.
- This will not only set up further memory links to your material, but will also give you the confidence that you can deliver your lines regardless of circumstances.

CHAPTER 8

CONTEXTUAL FACTORS FOR MEMORIZATION

THE IMPORTANCE OF CONTEXT

In the previous chapters, you have learned a variety of tools to get the lines securely embedded in your long-term memory.

Once that part of the process is complete, it is time to introduce variations in the context in which you rehearse your lines.

The more variations in context you can introduce as part of your memorization process, the more confident you can be that you will remember your lines regardless of circumstances.

In addition, with each variation in context, you will build even more memory links to the material.

We will discuss varying the environment in

which you memorize your lines, your physical activities, as well as the presence of others.

We will also discuss how to memorize dialogue, and how to deal with the context of the other actor's lines.

VARY YOUR MEMORIZATION ENVIRONMENT

One feature of memory is that as you start memorizing a piece of text, remembering it will be tied to your environment.

For example, if you memorize your lines in your bedroom, you will initially only remember your lines if you are in your bedroom.

This creates a problem for actors.

It makes them think they know their lines because they can remember them easily in one environment.

However, if that is the only environment in which they have spoken their lines, they may draw a blank when delivering their lines in the audition room.

Indeed, studies show that we remember something more easily in the environment in which we memorized it.

In one study, scuba divers were asked to memorize a list of unrelated words either on a boat or under water.

They were later asked to remember the words in either the same or a different environment in which they had been memorizing.

The results showed that what was learned in the water was best recalled in the water and vice versa.

You should therefore ensure that after you are comfortable with your lines, you start varying the environment and the circumstances in which you say them.

This will prevent you from getting a mental block when you have to deliver the lines in a different environment.

ALTERNATIVE TO VARYING THE ENVIRONMENT

In cases when you do not have enough time to vary the environment in which you learned your lines, there is a handy alternative.

You may be able to mentally recreate the initial environment in your mind as you are saying the lines in a different environment.

In one study, participants were presented with a long list of words.

A day later they were brought back for an unexpected recall test that took place in either the same room or one that varied in size, furnishings, etc.

The participants who were tested in the same location were considerably better at remembering the list of words than the participants who were tested in a different room.

However, a third group were also brought into the new room.

This third group of participants were asked to think about the room in which they had originally learned the list.

They were asked to think about what it looked and felt like.

The results showed that the third group performed no worse than the participants who were tested in the same room.

This suggests that if you do not have the time to vary the memorization environment, you should attempt to recreate it in your mind as best you can when saying the lines.

VARY YOUR PHYSICAL ACTIVITIES

We briefly discussed physical activities in the previous chapter.

In that chapter, I suggested that one way to build more memory links is to say your lines while doing a variety of physical activities as you go about your day.

However, in this section I would like to draw your attention to specific physical activities you may be doing while learning your lines without realizing, and that may get in the way.

The problem with such physical activities is that your brain may come to associate them with saying the lines, in the same way that muscle memory works.

For example, some actors enjoy pacing around the room while learning their lines.

You may also find it easier to learn your lines with your eyes closed, or while waving your hands around.

If any of these sound familiar, this is something you need to take into account.

There is nothing wrong with doing these things while you are memorizing, if this is helping you with the process.

However, once you have learned your lines, make sure you can say them without doing these things.

For example, if you pace while learning your lines, make sure you can also say your lines while standing still.

If you memorized while keeping your eyes closed, make sure you can say your lines with your eyes open.

The same thing goes for waving your hands around, or anything else that falls in this category.

The easier your lines come to you when you are not doing your habitual physical activities, the more certain you can be you won't draw a blank when it matters most.

THE PRESENCE OF OTHERS

One major contextual factor while saying your lines is the presence of others.

As you start saying your lines from memory, after the initial stages of memorization are over, you are probably on your own.

That is initially a good thing.

You are still letting the lines sink into your long-term memory.

The presence of others at that point would be an unhelpful distraction.

However, it is important you do not think you are done with your memorization process once you can say the lines to yourself.

After you feel completely confident saying your lines, find friends and family who are willing to run lines with you.

If you can, say your lines in front of several people, not just one person.

People who are restless and unenthusiastic about your request for help are particularly good to have among your trial audience members.

The less impacted you are by your audience's mood, the more confident you can be that you truly know your lines.

MEMORIZING DIALOGUE

In most cases, the lines you have to learn as an actor are part of a dialogue.

If so, one important contextual factor are the lines of the other actor(s).

When memorizing dialogue, I suggest you start by only learning your own lines.

Once you are able to say your lines completely

from memory and do all the things I suggested in the previous chapters, it is time to start taking into account the other lines that are part of the dialogue.

To do so, record yourself saying all the lines, including those of the other actor(s).

In case you are wondering, this is a separate recording to the one suggested in the previous chapter.

In that initial recording, you were only focusing on your own lines.

This second recording is for you to become accustomed to hearing the lines of the other actor(s) interspersed with your own lines, as they are in the script.

Listen to the recording as often as possible and say your lines when they come up, as if you were rehearsing with the other actor.

This will help you get used to saying your own lines and hearing the other lines (the ones you don't have to say) before/after yours in sequence.

As a result, you won't be thrown off when you have to listen out for the other actor's lines.

Indeed, it would be best if you could make two recordings: one at normal speed, the other at break-neck speed.

This means that if the other actor introduces a quicker pace while saying their lines, you are not thrown off.

First get used to the normal-paced version, then move on to the fast-paced one.

KEY POINTS

- In the initial stages of memorization, remembering is linked to the environment where you learned your lines.
- Once you can say your lines from memory, start varying the environment in which you say them.
- If varying the environment isn't possible, you can mentally recreate the memorization environment while delivering your lines.
- Remember to also take into account other contextual factors.
- Consider your physical habits while memorizing. These may include pacing around the room, keeping your eyes closed, or waving your hands.

Make sure you can remember your lines when you are not doing these things.

- Ask family and friends to run lines with you, to get used to saying your lines in front of others.

- To memorize dialogue, make recordings that include the other actor's lines.

- Vary the speed of the recording, so you do not get thrown off if the other actor says their lines quicker than you are used to and forces you to speed up your delivery.

CHAPTER 9

HOW TO SCHEDULE YOUR MEMORIZATION SESSIONS

THE STRATEGY OF TIME

There is a close connection between remembering and time.

As such, the way you schedule your memorization sessions plays an important part in how quickly you can learn your lines.

If you have never considered this topic, you may not realize that you can make your line learning process dramatically more efficient by using time as your ally.

This means you can spend less time learning your lines, yet remember them better than ever before.

To do so, you need to schedule your memorization sessions strategically.

Before we get into the detail of scheduling your sessions, let us first examine an important aspect of memorization: forgetting.

THE FORGETTING CURVE

Studies show that forgetting follows a certain pattern, called the 'forgetting curve'.

This curve shows that we forget the most right after we have learned something.

After this initial sharp decline in what we can remember, the curve becomes less steep, and then levels off.

If you are a stage actor and you have to memorize an entire play, do not rely on the rehearsal period to learn your lines.

Start memorizing some time before rehearsals begin.

As you forget the most after you have just learned the material, what works best is if you schedule the next session soon after the first.

You can then gradually increase the time between subsequent sessions.

Indeed, research shows that reviewing the

material at regular intervals increases your ability to remember it.

Over time, less frequent review is needed.

This has been termed the 'spacing effect'.

The more you take advantage of this effect, the more efficient your memorization sessions will become.

USING TIME AS AN ALLY

There are several other advantages of allowing time to elapse between memorization sessions.

Spacing memorization sessions over a longer period allows you to focus on the material at different times and in different circumstances.

This means you have the benefit of different things happening in your environment each time you memorize the material.

You may learn your lines in the morning, when the sun is shining, and again at night, when it is dark and cold.

These different circumstances provide more triggers for you to remember your lines.

For example, you may remember the ray of sunshine that hit you in the face just as you were saying a particular sentence.

By contrast, when you condense your memorization sessions into a short amount of time, what happens in your environment is likely to be similar with each repetition.

As such, you cannot benefit from these added memory triggers.

When you space out your memorization sessions, your brain also gets more opportunities to rehearse the material without your conscious awareness.

By contrast, when you do your memorization sessions within a short period, repeating the material over and over is likely to become boring.

As such, your brain is likely to be less engaged every time you go through the material.

You are therefore in danger of overestimating the extent to which you have learned the lines.

Having to memorize over a short period is also often accompanied by stress, which by itself has a negative effect on your ability to memorize.

Another advantage of spacing your memorization sessions over a longer period is due to the benefits of sleep on memory.

While you sleep, your brain is processing the lines, transferring them from short-term to long-term memory.

There are different explanations for why sleep helps with memorization.

One possibility is that when you are awake, you get bombarded with distractions.

These interfere with the process of allowing the material to take hold in long-term memory.

However, during sleep, memories can be consolidated without any obstacles.

Another explanation is that newly learned memories are reactivated during sleep.

This leads to them becoming more reliably stored in long-term memory.

Due to the positive effect of sleep on memorization, two of the best times to schedule your memorization sessions are before you go to sleep and after you wake up.

By rehearsing the lines before going to sleep, you are ensuring that the subconscious part of your brain will keep processing the material while you are sleeping.

Scheduling another session after waking up re-establishes the material at the forefront of your consciousness.

Your refreshed brain can then access this material and keep processing it throughout your day.

If you enjoy taking naps, you could build even more memorization sessions into your day.

You could work on your lines before and after each nap, and gain an excellent excuse for napping as part of this arrangement.

MEMORIZING UNDER TIME PRESSURE

There is a caveat to all this.

If the time between when you get the script and when you must remember it is short, scheduling your memorization sessions close together works better.

The brief amount of time does not allow you to fully transfer the material from short-term into long-term memory.

However, it does keep the lines at the forefront of your mind.

This ensures they remain accessible in the short-term.

As such, if you get your script the day before the audition, schedule your memorization sessions as close together as possible, especially near the time of your audition slot.

If you are forced to schedule your memorization sessions close together, here is a handy trick to keep your brain actively engaged despite the tedium of repetition: re-print your lines in different fonts every time you attempt to learn them.

One study demonstrated that changing the font in which repeated presentations of non-words were shown helped the learning process.

This was particularly the case when the material was presented at closely scheduled intervals.

This is because, as already discussed, the more engaged you are with the material, the more in-depth you are likely to process it.

In this case, changing the font forced partici-pants to pay more attention than when the text was presented in the same font every time.

In the same way, seeing your lines in a different font every time forces your brain to pay more attention.

This will speed up your memorization process, which is particularly important when you have a tight deadline.

KEY POINTS

- There is a general trend for how forgetting works.

- You tend to forget the most right after the initial memorization session, then there is a gradual leveling off.
- If you have lots of time before you have to deliver your lines, it is best to schedule your initial memorization sessions close together, then gradually space them out.
- Spacing your memorization sessions also allows you to take advantage of your subconscious consolidating your lines without any conscious effort, especially during sleep.
- If you have to learn your lines within a short time frame, it is best to schedule your memorization sessions close together.
- This will keep the lines at the forefront of your short-term memory.
- You can also print out your lines in different fonts for each session.
- This will help you pay closer attention while memorizing and keep your brain engaged with the lines all the way through.

CHAPTER 10

DEVELOPING THE RIGHT MINDSET

THE FEAR FACTOR

Your goals and beliefs as you memorize your lines are of crucial importance.

Usually, actors see learning lines as a chore to be completed so they can get on with the fun stuff: acting.

Their motivation for learning lines is often fear.

This motivation is based on solid ground.

If you do not learn your lines, you will not get the chance to show off your acting.

Even worse, forgetting your lines in front of a casting director may damage your chances in the future.

Why should they waste their time to call you in for an audition if they cannot be certain you will come fully prepared?

Casting directors are notoriously short on time but have an exceedingly good memory for people.

However, studies show that having fear as your primary motivation for completing a task is problematic.

Let us briefly discuss why you should avoid using fear as a motivation.

EXTRINSIC VS INTRINSIC MOTIVATION

Fear is a type of motivation psychologists call 'extrinsic'. It comes from outside yourself.

Extrinsic motivation works great for routine tasks which require minimal thinking or attention, such as sealing envelopes, factory work, or scanning items.

As the task does not require thinking and is tedious and repetitive, it makes sense to use extrinsic motivators such as fear to get it done.

You are more likely to put in your hours sealing envelopes if a supervisor is watching than if you were left to your own devices.

Learning lines is a tedious, repetitive task too, you may say.

However, compared to sealing envelopes, it is more complex and requires far more brain power on your part.

As such, your fear of embarrassment may only kick in when it is too late to give yourself enough time to prepare, rather than being there from the start.

A far more effective way to motivate yourself to learn lines is to use what psychologists call 'intrinsic motivation'.

This is a type of motivation that comes from within yourself.

Instead of learning lines because you fear the wrath of the casting director, or of the audience, what if you learned lines because the activity is fun and rewarding in itself?

Learning lines, fun?

It can be, if you frame it in a positive way.

MAKING MEMORIZATION FUN

To make memorization fun, start with the attitude that you *can* learn your lines.

If you hold a belief such as 'my memory is

poor', this is likely to become a self-fulfilling prophecy.

Instead, remember what you have learned towards the beginning of this book.

All healthy adults are perfectly equipped to memorize around seven items.

Unless you have dementia or anything similar, chances are your memory is absolutely fine.

The more you get into the habit of learning lines, the more of an 'expert' you will become at this task.

This is the same as how Steve Faloon became an expert at memorizing lists of random digits: through lots of practice.

To motivate yourself to keep practicing, you can make memorizing lines fun.

You can turn the process of memorization into something you enjoy, instead of treating it as a means to an end.

Don't just wait to get an audition to start learning lines.

Make it a habit to learn monologues or scenes in your spare time.

That way, learning lines for when the big day comes will not be daunting.

You can make this fun by keeping a tally score

on your wall of how many pieces you have learned in a set amount of time.

Give yourself targets and turn it into a game.

If you are a sociable person, you may enjoy learning lines more if you post your progress on social media, or if you ask a friend to help you.

Get into the mindset that learning lines is a fun activity that is rewarding in and of itself, rather than a chore to be done to avoid embarrassment.

The more fun and rewarding your memorization sessions are, the more likely you are to learn the lines well.

You will no longer be tempted to spend the minimum amount of time on the task and then blame your poor memory for drying up in auditions.

Overall, learning lines is like going to the gym.

If you only go to the gym once in a while, you cannot compare yourself to the guys with the big muscles.

However, these people were once the same as you.

They had to start from scratch and work their way up.

If you wanted to emulate their success, you

would probably start with some basic exercises first.

You would also start going to the gym regularly, and gradually increase the difficulty of your exercises.

It is the same with learning lines.

Trust that as you put the memorization process outlined in this book into practice, learning lines will gradually become easier and more fulfilling.

KEY POINTS

- Actors often rely on fear of embarrassment or similar kinds of 'extrinsic motivation' to learn their lines.
- However, as memorization is a complex task, using 'intrinsic motivation' (coming from inside oneself) is more effective and fulfilling.
- You can enhance your intrinsic motivation for memorization through employing the highly effective (and therefore motivating) tools and suggestions outlined in this book.

- You also need to challenge any negative beliefs you may hold about your memory capacity.
- Other intrinsically motivating factors include memorizing lines for its own sake, because it is a desirable skill to master, rather than to achieve a particular end-result.
- You can also turn memorization into a fun activity, for example by keeping tally scores of your memorization goals.
- Effective and reliable memorization is a learnable skill and you *will* get better at it the more you practice.

CHAPTER 11

A COHERENT
MEMORIZATION PROCESS

TAKE OWNERSHIP OF YOUR PROCESS

Having gone through all the tools you can implement to learn your lines easier and faster, it is time to put together a coherent memorization process.

This will allow you to see, at a glance, what approaching a piece of text might look like using the tools outlined in this book.

Of course, you are a unique individual.

As such, it is important that you take ownership of the memorization process you end up using for the long-term.

Only use my suggestions as a starting point for developing your own memorization process.

Having said that, the next few sections will outline the broad steps you may wish to follow.

DEEPEN YOUR ENGAGEMENT WITH THE TEXT

Start by reading the piece two or three times, from beginning to end.

Look up any unknown words or phrases.

You may also want to paraphrase to yourself the meaning of particularly tricky passages.

Make sure you memorize the actual lines rather than the paraphrased version.

ORGANIZE THE TEXT INTO CHUNKS

Divide the text into segments that are short enough for you to start memorizing one by one, i.e. 'chunk' the material to be memorized.

Remember you are aiming for seven chunks.

If the length of the piece means the initial chunks are too long to be used as a starting point, further divide each chunk into seven smaller ones.

Keep doing this until the size of each chunk feels manageable to you.

Take the first chunk.

Read through it out loud once or twice.

Make sure you understand what it means.

Look up any unfamiliar words or phrases.

Rehearse it several times until you can say it without looking at the text.

Try writing it out from memory several times.

Repeat this with each of the other chunks.

USE RETRIEVAL CUES TO MEMORIZE YOUR CHUNKS

Identify a retrieval cue for each chunk.

Try to pick retrieval cues that are memorable to you.

Make a list of your retrieval cues.

Put your page with the text next to you, but make sure it is not too easily visible.

Next, put your list of retrieval cues in front of you.

Try to say the text from memory while only looking at your retrieval cues.

Did that work?

If it didn't, go back to those chunks you had trouble with.

Rehearse these chunks a few more times individually before returning to the text as a whole.

Once you can say the entire text with only the help of the retrieval cues, put the text away.

Keep your list of retrieval cues close, but not too visible.

Try saying the text without looking at your retrieval cues.

Whenever you get stuck, allow yourself to look at the retrieval cue.

As your memorization process progresses, increase the size of your chunks.

By the end, you should only have seven chunks and seven retrieval cues, no matter how long the text.

You should also be able to easily remember your chunks without needing to look at the retrieval cues.

ESTABLISH MULTIPLE MEMORY LINKS TO THE MATERIAL

i) Write the lines down

Do this while memorizing individual chunks as well as towards the end, after you feel comfortable with the extent to which you have memorized the whole piece.

.   .   .

ii) Record yourself

Make two recordings of yourself reading the lines: one at normal speed, the other at breakneck speed.

Listen to the recordings as many times as you can.

Gradually try to say the piece at the same time as the recording.

First go with the normal-paced version, then move on to the fast-paced one.

Listening to the recording a few times before going to bed encourages your subconscious to continue the learning process while you sleep.

You will notice the results the next day, when picking up the piece again.

iii) Sing the lines to yourself

Singing distracts you from rhythms you may have developed while memorizing.

Change the tune regularly to keep the text fresh.

iv) Introduce distractions while saying the lines.

Once you know your lines, try saying them at breakneck speed.

Also try saying them while doing a wide range of physical activities such as moving furniture, riding a bike, or doing press-ups.

Do not assume you have finished your memorization until you are able to say the lines while doing something else at the same time.

CONSIDER CONTEXTUAL FACTORS

Once you are confident you have memorized your lines, start varying the environment in which you say them.

Say the lines in a different room.

Go for a walk while saying the lines.

Mutter the lines to yourself while waiting for the bus.

If you do not have enough time to vary the location, try to re-create the original context in your head before saying the lines in the audition room.

Consider other contextual factors that were tied to learning the lines.

If you memorized your lines while pacing around the room, make sure you can say them with just as much ease while standing still.

Similarly, if you memorized the lines while being on your own, make sure you can easily deliver them in front of family and friends.

When memorizing dialogue, initially only memorize your own lines.

Then make a recording of all the lines, including those of the other actor(s).

This will help you get used to hearing the other lines (the ones you don't have to say) before/after yours in sequence.

TURN TIME INTO YOUR ALLY

For best results, give yourself as much time as possible for memorizing and space out your memorization sessions.

If you can, start the memorization process as early as possible after being given your lines.

This will allow your brain to process the material while you sleep.

If you have the luxury of time, schedule your initial memorization sessions close together, then gradually space them out.

If you have to learn your lines in a short amount of time, schedule your memorization sessions close together, to keep the text at the forefront of your mind.

In addition, print out your text using a different font for each memorization session.

This will keep your brain engaged with the material and allow you to make the most of your available time.

DEVELOP A POSITIVE MINDSET

Approach memorization with a 'can do' attitude.

As you set about to start memorizing a new piece of text, challenge any negative beliefs you may have about your memorization abilities.

You have the same short-term memory capacity of around seven items as everyone else, including people who appear to have 'exceptional memories'.

You *can* memorize this text, and easily remember it, if you are prepared to put in the time it requires to do so.

In addition, unlike many actors, you now have a highly effective memorization process at your disposal: this book.

All you have to do is show up and do the work.

CONCLUSION

Congratulations!

You now have all the tools to become a master at learning your lines.

I hope the information and the suggestions you have gathered from this book will help you develop a bullet-proof memorization process.

As I have mentioned throughout this book, keeping your brain engaged with your lines amidst the tedium of repetition is key to how quickly and easily you can memorize.

Therefore, it is essential to find ways to best keep yourself actively engaged.

You are unique, and therefore, you have to make sure that the memorization process you use takes your uniqueness into account.

I hope that the tools I have provided here will give you lots of ideas for what you might like to try.

If anything I have suggested does not work for you, please ignore it.

Just keep the suggestions that work.

Thank you for sticking with me through this entire book.

I look forward to seeing you take the acting world by storm!

I would like to ask you for a small favor.

Reviews are the best way to spread the word about this book.

If you have found this book helpful, it would mean a lot to me if you could leave a review.

Even if you write only a sentence or two, it will help. Thank you!

ABOUT THE AUTHOR

Alexa Ispas holds a PhD in psychology from the University of Edinburgh.

She developed the memorization process outlined in this book while pursuing acting as a career after finishing her academic studies.

She eventually trained and worked as an energy healer and is currently writing books in her *Energy Awareness Series.*

If energy awareness interests you, feel free to check out Alexa's other books at

www.alexaispas.com

Made in United States
Orlando, FL
09 February 2022

14628372R00071